# "MAMA, LOOK!"

## Francis A Nimako

TO : Rosenbergs

ISBN: **0615484565**
ISBN-13: **978-0615484563**

Oh my friends!
Listen to
a story
I want
to
tell you.

Here comes a young, handsome, happy Grasshopper.

He was going for a walk in the field.

It was a beautiful
sunny day.

He was

so happy

because he had

finished his

work.

Spider was hot

and very tired from playing in

the bright sun

and asked Grasshopper,

"Do you have

a handkerchief?

"YEAH,

I have enough to give you!"

answered Grasshopper

Spider took the handkerchief

and

thanked Grasshopper,

crawling away to go play.

The rooster
didn't like

the always-happy
Grasshopper.
He wanted
Grasshopper
as his food.

# Rooster

would much rather
eat Grasshopper
than see him

happily hopping

all the time.

Out of the bush the rooster jumped on the

Grasshopper

and stared at him hungrily. Grasshopper begged the rooster to spare his life, but the rooster didn't care.

Grasshopper

cried out loud for MERCY!

"Tserich Tserich Tserich!"

Spider, and
Grasshopper's other friends,
Cockroach, Frog and Goldfinch
were playing nearby and
heard his cries.
"Tserich" "Tserich"

They ran to save Grasshopper.

"Bite his leg,

bite his leg,

but not too much".

Rooster turned his head
and said,
"What did you say?"

Cockroach nervously
replied
"I am sorry",

and hid
under a rock.

He had to be careful

or Rooster

would eat him too!

Then Frog
croaked loudly
in Rooster's ears.

Rooster cried out
in fright.

"KooKROOKoo" "KooKROOKoo"

# The fighting upset Goldfinch

# who shouted

"Tweet Tweet Tweet"

"Perclekoree"

"Stop!!

We should be friends!"

The rooster said softly "Kookrookoo.

I am wrong.

I won't do that again".

Scratching his feet
in the dirt,
Rooster said

" I am sorry.

I understand.

We can be friends."

As the sunsets

# ABEBE OYE ABOA  (Grasshopper is an animal)

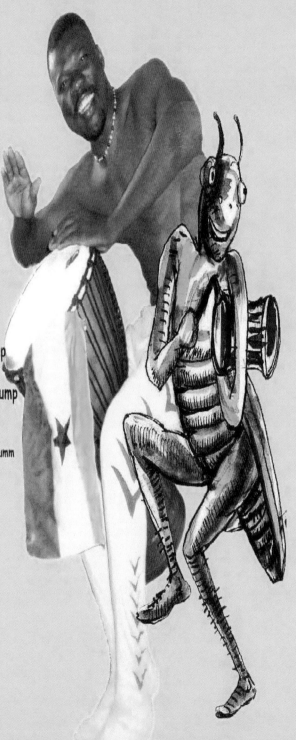

(2x)  Abebe oye aboa. Abebe O!
Abebe oye aboa. Abebe O!
Abebe oye aboa. Abebe OOOO!
Mama hwe,  Eye Abebe!!!

(4x) Natural toy we play from mama look

(4x)  Abebe oye aboa. Abebe O!
Abebe oye aboa. Abebe O!
Abebe oye aboa. Abebe OOOO!
Mama hwe,  Eye Abebe!!!

If you wana hop   you should jump
You should jump jump   If you wana hop
You should jump   You should jump jump jump
If you wana hop    You should jump
You should jump jump jump  You should jump jump
You should jump jump jump
If you wana hop
Kofi hum....hum.....Felicia....hum  Emma.......hum humm....kofi... humm

(3x) Grasshopper is animal
Abebe OOOO!
Mama, look! Catch the grasshopper

(2x)      Abebe oye aboa. Abebe O!
Abebe oye aboa. Abebe O!
Abebe oye aboa. Abebe OOOO!
Mama hwe,  Eye Abebe!!!

(3x) Grasshopper is animal
Abebe OOOO!
Mama, look! Catch the grasshopper

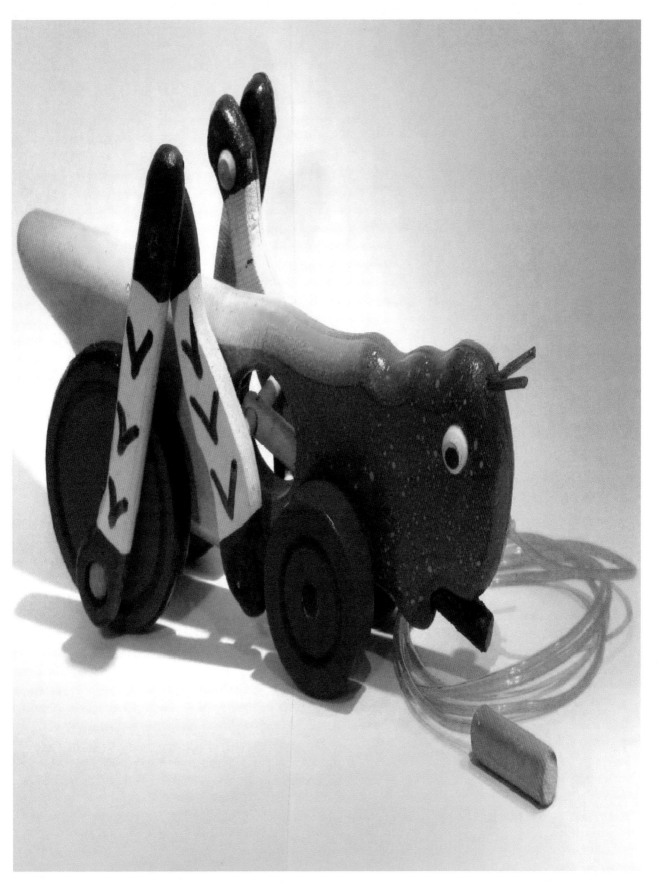

NORTH
AMERICA

EUROPE

ASIA

MIDDLE
EAST

AFRICA

SOUTH
AMERICA

AUSTRALIA

GHANA
WEST-AFRICA

Francis Nimako's was born in Ghana, West Africa where his creative imagination with wooden toys began.

As a young child in Ghana, Francis would call out "Mama, look!" as he playfully chased the many grasshopper and other animals, composing songs about them in his heart as he ran along. Hence, the name of his company "Mama, look!"

He fondly remembers the joy and laughter that the insects and animals, brought into his life and wants to educate children through sharing these memories. He seeks to bring the children of the world back to the nurturing simplicity of playing, singing, dancing and making music and nurturing through experiencing his wooden toys
However, his newest creation will reflect those elements into story books
Now he present to you his second Book called

" A YOUNG HANDSOME HAPPY GRASSHOPPER "

Made in the USA
Charleston, SC
04 June 2011